AFFIRMING

Martin Dudley

HUMANITY AND HEALING

The Ministry to the Sick
in the Catholic Tradition

Series Editor: Jeffrey John

DARTON · LONGMAN + TODD

First published in 1998 by
Darton, Longman and Todd Ltd
1 Spencer Court
140–142 Wandsworth High Street
London SW18 4JJ

in association with

Affirming Catholicism
St Giles Church
No 4, The Postern
Wood Street, The Barbican
London EC2Y 8BJ

ISBN 0–232–52272–3

The views expressed in this booklet are those of the
author and do not necessarily reflect any policy
of Affirming Catholicism

Designed by Bet Ayer
Phototypeset by Intype London Ltd
Printed and bound in Great Britain by
Page Bros, Norwich

Affirming Catholicism

Affirming Catholicism is a movement (not an ecclesiastical party) which exists to do two things. We affirm our confidence in our Anglican heritage; and we seek to renew and promote the Catholic tradition within it. Our aim is to explore, explain and share with others both inside and outside the Church a lively, intelligent and inclusive Catholic faith. In the words of our Trust Deed:

> It is the conviction of many that a respect for scholarship and free enquiry has been characteristic of the Church of England and of the Churches of the wider Anglican Communion from earliest times, and is fully consistent with the status of those Churches as part of the Holy Catholic Church. It is desired to establish a charitable educational foundation which will be true both to those characteristics and to the Catholic tradition within Anglicanism... The object of the foundation shall be the advancement of education in the doctrines and the historical development of the Church of England and the Churches of the wider Anglican Communion, as held by those standing within the Catholic tradition.

Our Publications

These are offered as one means of presenting Anglican Catholic teaching and practice in as clear and accessible a form as possible. Some cover traditional doctrinal and liturgical themes; others attempt to present a well-argued Catholic viewpoint on issues of debate currently facing the Church. There is a list of our series of booklets on page v.

The present series of books is provided, where appropriate, with summaries to sections, and suggested questions which we hope will facilitate personal study or discussion in groups. Other titles in the series are:

Christian Feminism – an Introduction Helen Stanton
Catholic Evangelism Stephen Cottrell

To order these publications individually or on subscription, or for further information about the aims and activities of Affirming Catholicism, write to:

The Secretary
Affirming Catholicism
St Giles Church
No 4, The Postern
Wood Street
The Barbican
London EC2Y 8BJ

Tel 0171 638 1980
Fax 0171 638 1997

Books in the Affirming Catholicism series

Affirming Confession John Davies

Catholicism and Folk Religion Jeremy Morris

By What Authority? – Authority, Ministry and the Catholic Church Mark D. Chapman

Christ in Ten Thousand Places – A Catholic Perspective on Christian Encounter with Other Faiths Michael Ipgrave

History, Tradition and Change – Church History and the Development of Doctrine Peter Hinchliffe

Imagining Jesus – An Introduction to the Incarnation Lewis Ayres

Is the Anglican Church Catholic? – The Catholicity of Anglicanism Vincent Strudwick

Is There an Anglican Way? – Scripture, Church and Reason: New Approaches to an Old Triad Ross Thompson

Lay Presidency at the Eucharist Benedict Green

'Making Present' – The Practice of Catholic Life and Liturgy Christopher Irvine

Marriage, Divorce and the Church Anthony E. Harvey

The Ministry of Deliverance Dominic Walker OGS

'Permanent, Faithful, Stable' – Christian Same-Sex Partnerships Jeffrey John

Politics and the Faith Today – Catholic Social Vision for the 1990s Kenneth Leech

Trinity and Unity Jane Williams

What is Affirming Catholicism? Jeffrey John

Why Women Priests? – The Ordination of Women and the Apostolic Ministry Jonathan Sedgwick

About the Author

Martin Dudley is Rector of the Priory Church of St Barthol-
omew the Great, Smithfield, in the City of London. Prior
to ordination in the Church in Wales, he studied theology
at King's College, London, and St Michael's College, Llan-
daff. His doctoral thesis was concerned with the crisis of
priestly identity in the Roman Catholic Church after
Vatican II.

He has been a parish priest for fifteen years and has
combined pastoral ministry with research in liturgy and
church history, teaching and writing. Secretary of the Alcuin
Club and a Fellow of the Society of Antiquaries and of the
Royal Historical Society, his publications include *The
Collect in Anglican Liturgy: Texts and Sources 1549–1989*
and *A Manual for Ministry to the Sick*.

Contents

Humanity, Health and Sickness 1
Biblical understandings of humanity 2
The medieval inheritance 4

The Anglican Tradition 12
The Book of Common Prayer 1662 12
The Alternative Service Book 1980 22
Charismatic healing 23
Various Anglican rites 24

The Roman Catholic Tradition 25
Developments after Vatican II 27
*Understanding sickness: rediscovering biblical
roots* 28

The Sacrament of the Sick 36
Who may receive the sacrament? 37
Who is the minister? 38
What is the right approach to the sacrament? 40
The 'matter' of the sacrament: the use of oil 42
How is the sacrament administered? 48
What is the effect of the sacrament? 49
*By what other means does the Church minister to the
sick?* 50

Conclusion 51
Questions 53
Further Reading and Resources 56

Humanity, Health and Sickness

What does it mean to be human? We need at least a preliminary answer to this question before it is possible to begin to consider healing. The answer might be that being human means living a short and rather brutal life, full of misery, dogged by illness, pain and adversity, a life of suffering from which we look forward to a happy release. Another answer would be that human life is about achieving physical, intellectual and emotional maturity, fulfilling the potential within us, and that sickness and pain are not an essential part of humanity. 'Being healed', in the first instance, might mean relief from the most severe pain or it might mean death; in the second, it might indicate being freed from physical and mental weakness. These are not the only answers; there are a great variety of them.

Most religions and many philosophies provide some answer to the meaning of our humanity. The Greek word *anthropos* signifies 'man', in the inclusive sense of 'humanity' and 'humankind'. In Genesis 1, God says, 'Let us make man in our own image'; the Greek word used to translate the Hebrew is *anthropos*. And the narrative continues: 'In the image of God created he them, male and female created he them.' 'Anthropology' is the word used to describe the study of humanity. We tend to think of it as the study of peoples who maintain tribal structures and tradition in Asia, Africa and South America, but it applies to any study that attempts to explain the meaning of our humanity. What I want to describe here is a variety of theological anthropologies: understandings of humanity based on an understanding of God. I am not looking to some remote theologians for this; as our source we will use our prayer books, ancient and modern, the rites that we use at crucial moments in our lives to mark birth, marriage, and death. We will find, perhaps inevitably, a considerable contrast between the books written in the reign of Edward VI that were revised to form *The Book of Common Prayer* 1662 and *The Alternative Service Book 1980*. More surprisingly, we will find just as great a contrast between the 1980 rites and what seems appropriate for the start of the next millennium. We could use birth and baptism to provide our insights, but we are here looking at the other extremity of life, at sickness and death.

Biblical understandings of humanity
The Old Testament writers do not set out to explain what it means to be human; instead they describe human beings as creatures of flesh and blood with needs and desires, socially involved in family, tribal and national relationships. We are given insights into certain aspects of life. If we follow the development of love, for example, in the book of Genesis we see that the first time someone is described as loving someone else it is the love of a father for his son.

God says to Abraham 'Take your son, your only son Isaac, whom you love . . .'. The next instance concerns Isaac: Abraham's servant brings him his kinswoman Rebekah and we are told that she became his wife, that he loved her, and that he was comforted after his mother's death. In the third occurrence Jacob seems to have fallen in love with Rachel as soon as he saw her tending the sheep. In these same chapters the covenant relation between God and humankind is set out, and we learn about the origins of toil, sexual desire, pain in childbirth, violence, and death. We find men and women set in communities with a commitment to one another that derives from their common relationship to God. The human being, created in the image of God, male and female, is like God in being pre-eminent among creatures, having the faculty of speech and knowing good and evil. But human beings are also destined to die, dust returning to dust. Genesis is rather matter-of-fact about it. Other books have a darker view. Though the psalmist frequently celebrates life, and especially the way in which the righteous flourish 'like a tree planted by a stream of water', yet it is also from the Psalms that we learn that the days of our age are threescore years and ten and our life but labour and sorrow, that we fade away suddenly like the grass. In most of the Old Testament writings there is at best little hope of an afterlife. *Sheol*, if it can be called a concept of the afterlife at all, is no more than a shadowy, enfeebled form of existence.

The Old Testament understanding of human disobedience and sinfulness carries over into the New Testament. Human beings are under judgement and are called by God to a radical conversion. Jesus also does not present some ideal version of what it means to be human. He addresses human beings in their concrete relationships to each other and to God. Both are to be characterised by love, and the commandment to love our neighbour as ourself is superseded by the new commandment, to love one another as Christ loves us. Jesus is forced, not least by the questions of the scribes and Pharisees, to address the issues raised by sexual desire, marriage and adultery, money and property, sickness and death. Those presented to Jesus are often sick or described as 'possessed by demons' and their hold on humanity sometimes seems rather tenuous. Sin, sickness and demonic possession efface the image of God; Jesus' healing word restores it and enables individuals to function again in a truly human way. But Jesus also points towards a new humanity which gives priority to service and to love of other people and embodies a deep care for those at the edges of society. He also affirms, against the mainstream of Old Testament thinking but in keeping with Daniel and the Pharisees, that death is the gateway to the infinitely richer eternal life of the resurrection.

The medieval inheritance
The English religious inheritance – meaning here the common inheritance of those who use the English language – derives not from the early Church but, by

way of the Authorised Version of the Bible and *The Book of Common Prayer*, from the Middle Ages. The medieval world view was not scientific. The understanding of humanity derived from revelation, from detailed commentary on Scripture. From it and from reflection upon the experience of life the medieval thinker, the poet, the artist, the preacher created a complex world very different from the one in which we live. We can glimpse it, for example, when we look at the sculptures adorning churches and cathedrals in France, the very heart of medieval culture. If we read medieval theologians, we will find a detailed discussion of the soul and its faculties and an evaluation of the body and its suitability in relation to the soul. We may well be struck by distinctions between soul and body familiar to us from often used prayers, or by distinctions between the material and spiritual elements of which we are made. We will also see a striking literalism of interpretation.

We need to focus our reflection, for several volumes could be devoted to medieval anthropology. It was not static; we can observe stages of development. The understanding of sickness and the sacramental and liturgical ministry to the sick and dying also changed and developed. Three tendencies in the life of the Church shaped this ministry in the period from apostolic times to the Reformation.

The first tendency identified the sick person with Christ. It clearly differentiated 'the sick' as a group of people from those who are not – or not yet – sick, 'the healthy'. This is not surprising. The Gospels clearly say that the sick and the possessed were brought to Jesus. Jesus himself said to the Pharisees: 'Those who are well have no need of a physician, but those who are sick.' And he continued: 'For I have come to call not the righteous but sinners' (Matthew 9:12–13, Luke 5:31–2). The Church has continued to maintain a distinction between the need of all people for salvation and wholeness and the quite specific need of the sick for healing and of sinners for forgiveness. The special place of the sick is well expressed in the Rule of St Benedict for monasteries: 'Before all else and above all else, care must be taken of the sick, so that they may be served as Christ himself in very deed, for he said: "I was sick and you visited me" and "What you did for the least of these you did for me." '

The second tendency came from an attempt to reconcile within the Church's life and teaching divergent understandings of sickness in relation to sin and punishment. The connection between sin and sickness is found in the Old Testament, which was the source of uch medieval practice. Though apparently denied by Jesus, it reappears in the letter of James. The anointing of the sick is specifically linked to confession of sins and the prayer of the Church for the sick is linked to forgiveness. Pope Gregory the Great expressed a view of sickness as a divine scourge, as a disciplining of the flesh, and as a means of being united to Christ in his suffering. This view remained current throughout the Middle Ages, and the relation of sin and sickness was specifically reaffirmed by the Fourth Lateran Council of 1215. The *First Prayer Book of King Edward VI*

(1549) continued this teaching, and it was carried into *The Book of Common Prayer* (1662).

The third tendency displayed a lack of confidence in any form of healing, other than miraculous means, and a recognition that death is inevitable. The power to heal was associated with magic, supernatural powers, and special religious gifts. A sick person was more likely to seek healing at the shrine of a saint than by consulting a physician. Medical science did not flourish during the Middle Ages and the Church may, in part, have been responsible for this. Medical theory was derived from classical writers, especially Hippocrates, Galen and the Persian Avicenna. Practice was based on theory, not on direct, clinical observation and the actual experience of sickness and health. Physicians rarely touched their patients. Surgeons, the next in the medical hierarchy, performed operations of various kinds and did bone-setting. Next came the barber-surgeons with no knowledge of pathology, physiology and epidemiology. Hospitals existed, of course, in the Middle Ages, but they were institutions designed to isolate the sick not to cure them.

The first tendency made the sick a group that required special attention. They received compassion but they were also marginalised. The rules of both St Augustine and St Benedict provided for an infirmarian to care for the sick. Such a specialised ministry guaranteed seriousness and efficiency but it also separated the majority of the monastic community from the suffering of Christ expressed in and through the sick. This was true in the wider community as well, yet both inside and outside religious houses it continued to be recognised that Christ's words were addressed to all. Confraternities with a particular ministry to the sick and dying expressed this wider ministry through their para-liturgical rites (e.g. the bringing of a holy candle, which was regarded as an efficacious symbol of hope and charity, especially in time of plague). The combination of the second and third tendencies led to the abandonment in the eighth century of the early Church's ministry of healing. There developed instead an elaborate rite of passage for the dying.

This ministry, liturgical and sacramental, could be divided into five parts. The first part, the general visitation of the sick, involved the presence of a priest and other ministers, members of the family and possibly members of devout confraternities. Paintings of that period depicting the sick in bed show the ministers with crucifix, candles, incense and holy water. They also show the presence of other beings, angels or devils depending on the eternal destiny of the deceased. The rite included the penitential psalms and the litany. The second element was confession, together with the absolution of excommunicants who had repented. Hugh of St Victor urged the baptised not to leave repentance to the last moment, to the deathbed 'when pain binds the limbs and grief oppresses the sense', but he affirmed that it was better late than never, and promised that a person who did then repent truly went forth 'in firm hope with the pledge of good devotion.' Third, the sacrament of extreme unction was the last of the anointings given to Christians, and fourth, the 'food for the journey', viaticum, was the last reception of holy communion. In the final part, the watch with the dying person, the departing soul was commended before the corpse of the deceased was taken from the house.

In 1273, the Synod of Evreux, concerned that all who died should be prepared for salvation, decreed that 'If anyone, young or old, because of the fault, negligence, or absence of his priest dies without baptism, confession, reception of the Body of the Lord, and extreme unction, the priest so convicted is to be suspended from the celebration of the divine mysteries. . . .'

The rites, and changes in them, can be documented from liturgical sources, but also, and more vividly from medieval stories, letters and lives of the saints. In Bede's life of Cuthbert, written about 721, the saint received 'the sacraments that lead to eternal life'. This apparently meant the Lord's body and blood but not anointing. Charlemagne also received holy communion, but was not anointed, and anointing is absent, too, from the death accounts in the medieval stories of the Knights of the Round Table. Peter the Venerable's letter to Héloïse on the death of Abelard (1142) details his profession of faith, confession of sin, and reception of the viaticum, followed by the commendation of his soul. There is no anointing. Abbot Peter does say, however, that all Abelard's brothers in religion and the whole monastic community can bear witness to the manner of his death, implying that many of them were gathered at his deathbed. Paintings of the death of the Virgin, of St Benedict, St Francis, and of other saints, show us these deathbed gatherings. In a similar way William of St Thierry's *Vita Prima* of St Bernard (1145–8) describes Bernard hearing the confession of the knight Josbert of La Ferté-sur-Aube, made with tears and sighs, and giving him the sacrament, i.e. the body of Christ. Again there is no anointing, but in William Daniel's *Life of Aelred*, begun shortly after 1167, we read that Aelred 'was anointed with holy oil by Roger, the venerable abbot of Byland, and was fortified by the viaticum of the most sacred body and blood of Our Lord, which he received with tears,' and John of Ford tells us, after 1181, that Wulfric, the recluse of Haselbury made his confession to the priest Osbern and 'having received absolution from the priest, he was fortified according to rite with the other sacraments of the Church.' This suggests that during the latter half of the twelfth century it became normal to administer extreme unction.

An idealised version of the rites is given in Bernard Gui's *Life of St Thomas Aquinas* (1274) in which the dying theologian calls for the viaticum, then makes the profession of faith 'as the Church discipline requires' and the next day asks to be anointed. His mind, we are told, remained clear throughout the ceremony and he answered the prayers himself. Then he joined his hands and gave back his Spirit to his Maker.

The importance of deathbed confession is apparent in the first story from Boccaccio's collection called the *Decameron* (begun by 1350) in which two Florentine brothers have to resolve the problem of what to do with the notorious sinner, Ser Ciappelletto, who has fallen ill in their house. They cannot evict a dying man for fear of public opinion but they doubt either that he would be willing to make his confession or receive the sacraments; and if he dies unconfessed, no church will receive his body. Even if he did make confession, no one would absolve him and the result would be the same. The sick man himself resolves the problem, deceives an old and holy friar, makes his confession and then asks him to send 'that true body of Christ which you consecrate every morning on the altar' and afterward 'to receive the holy Extreme Unction, so that, having lived as a sinner, I shall die as a Christian.' He receives communion and, failing rapidly, receives the anointing and dies.

The Anglican Tradition

At the time of the Reformation in England, little changed in the basic approach to the sick. It is summed up in the preface to 'The Communion of the Sicke' in 1549: 'Forasmuche as all mortal men be subject to many sodaine perils, diseases, and sicknesses, and ever uncertaine what time they shall depart out of this lyfe . . .' The Order of Visitation in 1549 included exhortation to steadfastness in faith, examination in the articles of faith, provision for a special confession, anointing (though only upon the head or breast and not on all the sense organs as had been previously the custom), and communion, brought from an open celebration in church. Special confession was retained in the Prayer Book of 1552 and in *The Book of Common Prayer*, but anointing was omitted and communion was no longer to be reserved or brought from the church; rather there was to be a celebration in the house.

The Book of Common Prayer 1662

We must now examine in greater detail the understanding of our humanity presented in the 1662 Prayer Book in which 'The Order for the Visitation of the Sick' follows directly after the Solemnization of Matrimony. Charles Wheatly (1686–1724), a learned commentator on the Prayer Book, did not think that this was accidental:

> In a world so full of casualties as this we live in, in which sickness and even death sometimes interrupts the marriage solemnities, it should be no matter of surprise that this melancholy office is placed immediately after that of matrimony. The eastern emperors thought it not unsuitable to choose the stone for their sepulchre on the day of their coronation. And it would not a little tend to temper and moderate the exuberant joys which sometimes attend the festivities of marriage, if by casting an eye on the following form, we should call to mind that the next and longer scene may be calamitous.

Wheatly is not just himself being melancholy. This rather mournful view expresses the prevailing sentiments of the Prayer Book. 'All men are conceived and born in sin' declares the 1662 service of infant baptism. Men and women come together in matrimony so that they may procreate, may avoid fornication, and may benefit, in prosperity and adversity from 'mutual society, help and comfort.' A man is to love his wife, and a woman is to be 'loving and amiable, faithful and obedient to her husband'. Fruitful procreation is to take place only within this union, which is not intended merely 'to satisfy men's carnal lusts and appetites' (here 'men' truly means both men *and* women). Conception brings women into the 'great pain and peril of Child-birth', into danger, for both mother and child. These difficulties are seen as the natural state (or at least the state after the sin of Adam and Eve). And if this was not enough, human beings, born of the flesh are *flesh* and so cannot be pleasing to God 'but live in sin, committing many actual transgressions.' Baptism 'with Water and the Holy Ghost' provides the regeneration that the flesh cannot otherwise have.

Baptism does not accomplish everything, and the baptised are urged to 'continually mortify' their 'evil and corrupt affections' and to live in a virtuous and godly way. The Prayer Book does not suggest that it will be easy. We see ourselves, barely saved from death, physical and spiritual, surrounded by great adversities, constantly assaulted by enemies, and in daily peril because of falling into sin and running into every kind of danger. The night, in particular, is full of perils and dangers. Manifold sins and wickedness appear to be the norm as we follow 'too much the devices and desires of our own hearts,' offending against God's laws, failing to do what we ought to have done and doing what we ought not to have done. Even if we do maintain the faith, there is always the risk of falling away from God, at the last hour, because of the pains of death.

Within this anthropology, sickness and death are a consequence of sin. Illness cannot be avoided; Wheatly says: 'it is certain that no age nor sex, no state nor condition, can secure us from sickness'. Its immediate causes are many. Sickness is 'God's visitation' sent either to try the person's patience 'for an example of others' and to test faith that it may receive a greater reward, or else it 'be sent unto you to correct and amend in you whatsoever doth offend the eyes of your heavenly Father'. Unworthy reception of the sacrament in holy communion provokes God 'to plague us with divers diseases and sundry kinds of death'. The only remedy is repentance, patient bearing of sickness, and humble submission to God. In the face of grave sickness the Prayer Book exhortation goes further in linking the individual's suffering to Christ's passion:

> And there should be no greater comfort to Christian persons, than to be made like unto Christ, by suffering patiently adversities, troubles, and sicknesses. For he himself went not up to joy but first he suffered pain; he entered not into his glory before he was crucified. So truly our way to eternal joy is to suffer here with Christ; and our door to enter into eternal life is gladly to die with Christ; that we may rise again from death, and dwell with him in everlasting life.

Death might not come in the present illness but it was inevitable, then as now. The Burial Office pushes home the idea – already surely apparent at the grave side – that 'man that is born of woman hath but a short time to live,' declares that 'in the midst of life we are in death' and that life, anyway, is 'full of misery'. Death is described as *dissolution*; the dissolving of the union between soul and body or as departure of the soul from the body. The best Christian hope could offer at this point was that, while our bodies lay in the dust, our souls would rest in God. As death is inevitable and sickness its unpleasant prelude, life short and full of misery, the Prayer Book's anthropology has little time for joy and little thought of healing. If a person is healed, it is because of God's will.

Human nature may not change but the way in which we perceive it and understand it does. Between 1662 and the present day stand some of the greatest movements in human thought: the Enlightenment and the French Revolution, the scientific revolutions, the advance of theories of evolution, the increased understanding of the workings of the human mind, and the discovery of DNA and the genetic structure. We still recognise aspects of our humanity in the language and the services of the Prayer Book but its anthropology is not ours. By the end of the nineteenth century there was a desire to express a new understanding in and through the Church's rites. The ministry to the sick gained particular attention.

The 1908 Lambeth Conference, in its Report on Ministries of Healing, pointed out that the 1662 services for the ministry to the sick did not adequately represent and might even be said to misrepresent the mind of the Church on sickness. The Lambeth Conference of 1920 considered healing in relation to the rise of Christian Science. Mary Baker Eddy (1821–1910) claimed a remarkable healing experience after a fall in 1866 through which she was led to the discovery of how to be well and of how to heal others. In 1875 she produced the book which would become the central authority of the Christian Science movement, *Science and Health with Key to the Scriptures*. Christian Science rests on a dualism which affirms spirit as being all that truly exists and matter as unreal illusion and nothing. Sickness is false belief existing only in the human mind, and disease and illness can be removed by the prayer of spiritual understanding. The Conference's deliberations were also influenced by scientific developments, the most important of which was the awareness that bacteria carry disease. The increase in health and life-expectancy before the 1930s was for the most part due to hygiene and sanitation policies introduced because of this new awareness. The Conference resolutions expressed thankfulness 'for the devoted labours of those engaged in scientific research and for the progress made in medicine, surgery, nursing, hygiene and sanitation' and the belief 'that all these means of healing and preventing disease and relieving suffering are gifts that come from God'. It also asked the Archbishop of Canterbury to appoint a committee to consider and report upon the use with prayer of the laying-on of hands, of the unction of the sick and other spiritual means of healing. The committee issued its highly influential report *The Ministry of Healing* in 1924 at a time when prayer book revision was taking place. The House of Clergy called for the inclusion of both unction and the laying-on of hands in the revised book. The bishops were unwilling to commit themselves until after the 1930 Lambeth Conference and so the 1928 book in England made no provision for anointing, though the 1929 revisions in America and Scotland did.

The 1930 Lambeth Conference commended the 1924 report and, in Resolution 73, said:

(b) Methods of Spiritual Healing, such as Unction or the Laying-on of Hands, should be used only in close conjunction with prayer and spiritual preparation.

(c) There is urgent need for co-operation between clergy and doctors since spiritual and physical treatment are complementary and equally necessary for true well-being.

(d) Seeing that the ministry of the Church is a ministry for the whole man, it is of utmost importance that the clergy should equip themselves for a fuller understanding of the intimate connexion between moral and spiritual disorders and mental and physical ills.

In 1932 Charles Harris wrote of other factors that had given rise to a renewed interest in healing: more careful study of Christ's attitude to disease and of the Church's actual exercise of the ministry of healing in apostolic, primitive and medieval times; uneasiness about insanity and nervous diseases; the rise of the New Psychology (Freud, Jung, Adler); medical recognition of the moral and spiritual aspects of disease; pastoral experience where rites of anointing were already in use, and the rise of Christian Science. The 1939 Report of the 1922 Doctrine Commission was still cautious about commending anointing, though it believed it could be seen as an outward and visible rite which was a 'symbol of the grace of God for the strengthening of the body and soul in their weakness.'

It can seem, so often, that the Church talks and

talks about a matter, sets up commissions, writes reports, and does nothing. The reason, on this occasion, is that it was not perceived as a pressing need. The dominant anthropology increasingly reduced the religious dimension in humanity; it was replaced by the psychological. Those who wanted to use anointing chose to do so for one of two reasons: either they were following Roman practice and wanting to use all the sacraments, or they saw it as a medicine that, after due preparation, could be administered like any other medicine. The 'Counsel to the Priest', appended to an order for 'Administration of Holy Unction and the Laying-on of Hands' issued by the Convocation of Canterbury in 1935, recommended that, if the ailment was mainly moral and spiritual or there was mental or nervous trouble, the priest should make several visits 'in order to diagnose accurately the nature and cause of the malady, and to determine in detail the spiritual treatment needed.' Moral and spiritual ailments had replaced the 'unruly wills and affections' of the Prayer Book.

In 1953, at a time of renewed hope, the archbishops set up a further commission which reported in 1958. The report, *The Church's Ministry of Healing*, offered a reaffirmation of the importance of this ministry which is, it said,

> an integral part of the Church's total work by which men and women are to become true sons and daughters of God's kingdom. In it are to be employed all the means God has put at our disposal: the administration of the Word and Sacraments; the exercise of pastoral care; and

the employment of all the gifts of special kinds which God has given to individuals.

It also set out some basic teachings, including a definition of healing as 'that which enables a person to function as a whole in accordance with God's will for them', and a set of misconceptions that are worth listing:

- Healing inevitably follows faith.
- Suffering is always contrary to God's will.
- God must heal.
- Death is a disaster.
- Sickness is always caused by sin.
- Modern medicine has superseded the Church's ministry of healing.
- The Church's ministry is in the hands only of the specially gifted.
- The Church's healing ministry is separate from its other work.
- Physical healing is all that matters.
- Sacramental ministries herald death.
- A medically unexplained healing is more wonderful than one brought about by medical means.

The 1958 Lambeth Conference began the serious process of incorporating the discussion of the previous fifty years into the newly begun process of liturgical renewal. The section on the ministry to the sick (within the section on revision of the BCP chaired by the Irish Primate, G.O. Simms, and with the liturgically-minded Bishop L.W. Brown from Uganda as secretary) began by stressing the need to remove erroneous assumptions about sickness (e.g. that God uses it for punishment). The Conference made the following proposal:

> In any future revision, seeing that every case of sickness requires its own treatment, the following outline is suggested:
> (a) The title 'Visitation of the Sick' should be altered to 'Ministry to the Sick', and be introduced by rubrics and directives bidding the priest (i) to minister to the whole person, whose soul and mind are involved as well as his sick body; (ii) to build up the hope and faith of the sufferer; (iii) to help him to put his affairs in order, and to be in love and charity with all men; and (iv) to move him to make his peace with God.
> (b) The following elements should be included in this section of the Prayer Book:
> (i) Passages of Scripture for reading and meditation.
> (ii) A form for the Laying-on of Hands.
> (iii) A form for Anointing.
> (iv) A form for the Communion of the Sick.
> (v) A form for Confession and Absolution of the Sick.
> (vi) A Commendation of the Dying.
> (vii) Various prayers and short litanies appropriate to different types of suffering.

The 1978 Conference clearly felt that all the Anglican Provinces (England among them) had not taken notice of this statement. Neglect of the ministry of healing diminished our part in Christ's total redemptive activity, declared the bishops, and ministry to the sick should be an essential element in any revision of the liturgy. It still took the Church of England until 1983 to provide such a form of ministry.

The Alternative Service Book 1980
It is amazingly difficult to locate an anthropology in the *ASB*. The purpose of our creation is declared, in a prayer from the marriage service, to be that of glorifying God 'in body and in spirit'. The thanksgiving for childbirth, however, says nothing about what it means to be human. The baptism of infants tells us that by the birth of children parents are given 'a share in the work and joy of creation'. Marriage is a gift of God in creation and leads to a bodily union which strengthens the union of the couple's hearts and lives, and there is a stress on so living now that we receive the blessings of eternal life. The funeral service repeats familiar words from *The Book of Common Prayer* reminding us (optionally) that life is short, though not suggesting that it is miserable. When we have sinned, it is through negligence, weakness, and our own deliberate fault, though it hardly seems to be a problem, for we are already in eternal life and need only to be kept in it and though there are still the assaults of our enemies and the power of our adversaries, plus the risk of falling into sin or running into danger, we are freed from the slavery of sin and counted as worthy to stand in the presence of God. The supplement containing ministry to the sick appeared in 1983 and is silent about the causes of sickness and the meaning of health. Though we offer

God our souls and bodies after communion we are offered no explanation of the relation between them. Rich in so many ways, the *ASB* lacks any real understanding of a sinful, suffering and ultimately redeemed humanity.

Charismatic healing

There were a number of organisations in England, like the Guild of St Raphael, advocating the normalisation of anointing and providing rites and commentaries, but meanwhile other types of healing became usual within the Christian community. Charismatic healing, deriving from the Pentecostal tradition, is very different to the liturgies of the sick. The Charismatic movement expects miracles. Miraculous healings do not need to be explained or excused. It is the absence of healing that needs explanation, for Scripture attests that there is a charismatic gift of healing (1 Corinthians 12:9, 28). This may be contrasted with the more 'official', quasi-liturgical concept of healing ministry in James 5, where it is linked with the official ministry of elders (presbyters): 'Is any among you sick? Let him call for the elders of the church, and let them pray over him, anointing him with oil in the name of the Lord.' Healing within the Charismatic movement is usually conceived in very full terms, not just physical ones, though physical healing is consciously sought and often experienced. Because of the inner nature of much healing, it is possible to assert that healing is taking place even without physical healing being evident, though this has been described as giving God the advantage of a 'Heads-I-win-tails-you-lose' analysis of whatever happens. Charismatics see a direct connection between Jesus' healing ministry and their own, but the evidence is not available to support this view.

Various Anglican rites
New rites for the sick were introduced in America (1979), England (1983 and 1991), Wales (1984), Canada (1985), New Zealand (1989), South Africa (1989) and Australia (1995). Within a general pattern conforming to that recommended by the 1958 Lambeth Conference they offer a variety of perspectives on the meaning of anointing. The prayers for blessing oil are usually more explicit in asking for the gift of healing than the rites of anointing are. Only the American rite stresses that the sacrament must be received in faith and repentance. Most of the rites speak of forgiveness, release from suffering, restoration to wholeness and strength. The Southern African rite makes much of protection from the assaults of evil and the powers of darkness. The New Zealand rite speaks of allowing the power of Christ to flow through the person anointed.

The Roman Catholic Tradition

We now turn to the Roman Catholic Church which, in the sixteenth century, shared with the Church of England the medieval inheritance and the emphasis on rites of the sick as a preliminary to death. The practice of anointing the sick retained by the Council of Trent gradually declined through the centuries. The Genoese priest Joseph Frasinetti (1804–68) was an exemplary pastor known as the 'Italian Curé d'Ars'. His manual for parish clergy first appeared in 1863 and after nine Italian editions it was translated into English. Well versed in theology, Frasinetti was also blessed with good pastoral sense. He acknowledges that in the average city parish of the late nineteenth century the priest will know nothing of the condition of the sick until he is called to administer the last rites. These, he says, should be administered in good time, but he knows that relatives, in order not to alarm the patient, delay too long in calling for the priest. There is no sense that anointing is a rite of healing; it is a preparation for dying. Frasinetti sees that this is not the original intention and lays down a pastoral principle:

> Extreme unction ought not to be administered at the last moment of life, but in every case of serious, and therefore dangerous, illness...[the parish priest] ought

to teach this doctrine not only in the church, but when he is visiting the sick: and he should impress it upon the sick persons themselves, upon their relatives, and especially upon the medical attendants.

The pocket editions of the *Rituale Romanum* contained the chapter *'De Visitatione et Cura Infirmorum'* as well as *'De Sacramento Extremae Unctionis'* with the rite of anointing in Latin. Parish priests often used a book of excerpts from the *Rituale* with some parts in the vernacular; these generally contained extreme unction and the form for commending a departing soul but no other form of ministry to the sick. The very briefest sacramental formulae, for emergency baptism, confession, unction and viaticum, were also printed on the last pages of the breviary. Writing in the mid-1960s in a major theological encyclopaedia a Catholic scholar declared:

> The sacramental anointing of the sick today holds little pastoral appeal. Sick people send for the doctor, not the priests. Only when medical science and skill fail, do they ask for the sacrament of the sick. This sacrament is considered as the herald of coming death and people keep away from it as long as possible. Even when presented as the sacrament of the sick, if not of healing, rather than as the sacrament of the dying, people find it hard to appreciate its precise role in the Christian life, the encounter with Christ proper to this sacrament. The difficulty may well be due not only to the modern outlook on life more intent on this world and inclined to ignore the next, but also to a defective pastoral presentation.

Developments after Vatican II

Notwithstanding lack of demand for this sacrament, after the Second Vatican Council the Roman Catholic Church produced a provisional rite of anointing and for pastoral care of the sick in Latin in 1972, with an interim English version in 1974 and a definitive version *Pastoral Care of the Sick* (hereafter *PCS*) in 1982. As with all the revised Roman rites, it has a general introduction explaining the theological and pastoral background to the rite. The new pastoral presentation involved a concerted effort to overcome the negative implications of the sacrament.

The Church's understanding of human sickness is set out in terms of the mystery of salvation. *PCS* begins by acknowledging that suffering and illness have always been among the greatest problems troubling the human spirit. This is true of all people, Christian and non-Christian. Christians, just like other people, feel and experience pain but their faith helps them to grasp more deeply the mystery of human suffering. From the words of Christ they know that sickness has meaning and value both in terms of their own salvation and that of the world in general. The Christian faithful also know that Jesus gave a special place to the sick during his earthly ministry, that he often visited them and healed them, and so they know that Christ loves them in sickness and suffering. In sickness, we experience our impotence, the limits of our existence and finitude, and in all sickness we catch a glimpse of death.

When we are attempting to establish a Christian

understanding of illness, language is particularly important. The 1982 version of *PCS* joins together 'suffering' and 'illness'; an earlier version spoke instead of 'sickness' and 'pain', and another translation of the introduction had 'illness' and 'pain'. There are important distinctions to be made here which have obviously troubled the translators and need some clarification. The first is between generalised suffering and sickness or illness. Sickness is an evil and does not belong to the original nature of humankind. It is to be distinguished from the sufferings to which people are exposed from without, such as hunger, exhaustion, and cold, and from inner trials, such as grief and other similar afflictions. There are also distinctions to be made between being ill, being sick, and being in pain. A number of these distinctions arise from the way in which we use words to label our own state at any given time and the state in which we find other people. In general, we can define 'illness' as a subjective and short-term state, and 'sickness' as a socially accepted category. The introduction to *PCS* makes 'the sick' a category of people within the Church who have a distinct role that includes fighting against illness and being helped to do so.

Understanding sickness: rediscovering biblical roots
The introduction to *PCS* affirms that sickness is closely linked to the human condition, that is to human sinfulness, but also states unequivocally that as a general rule sickness cannot be regarded as a punishment inflicted on an individual for personal

sins. John 9:3, in which Jesus denies that a man is blind because of his own sin or his parents' sin, is cited here. The new Roman Catechism develops this brief statement, beginning from those Old Testament passages in which sickness is closely associated with the idea of punishment. Psalm 38 is a key text with its declaration, 'there is no health in my bones because of my sin' (v. 3) – a text which was obviously used in writing the confession for Prayer Book Matins and Evensong. Not only does punishment come from God – Psalm 6:3 – but so does the possibility of healing (see the healing of Hezekiah in Isaiah 38). Seen in this way, sickness recalls a person to God, from whom must be sought the pardon that leads to healing. There are two aspects of sickness, therefore: it is related on the one hand to sin and evil, and on the other to fidelity to God. In Exodus 15:26 Moses assures the people that if they are obedient God will not bring upon them the diseases he brought upon the Egyptians. God also says to them, 'I am the Lord who heals you.' In Isaiah, suffering has a redemptive dimension, not only for the individual who suffers but for others as well. 'Surely he has borne our infirmities and carried our diseases,' says the prophet Isaiah (53:4) and he affirms, 'The righteous one, my servant, shall make many righteous, and shall bear their iniquities' (53:11). He also looks forward to another order of things: in the new Zion there will be no illness, 'And no inhabitant will say, "I am sick"; the people who live there will be forgiven their iniquity' (33:24).

The introduction, turning now to the New Testament, says that Christ, who was himself without sin, fulfilled the words of Isaiah and shared in all human pain by taking on the wounds inflicted in his passion. Christ still suffers whenever his followers suffer. Here, however, the confusion between 'suffering' and 'sickness' recurs. We have no record of Jesus being ill; his suffering was imposed upon him. The catechism acknowledges that there may be experiences that appear to contradict the good news of salvation, specifically evil and suffering, injustice and death. In these experiences God does not appear to be omnipotent. We are reminded that the power of God is manifested in a mysterious and incomprehensible way in the passion and resurrection of Christ, events which led to the conquest of evil. We must not expect to understand the divine mysteries. In the original paradise, the Garden of Eden, there was neither death nor suffering; both came as a consequence of sin. The grace of God in baptism effaces this original sin and returns humankind to God but the consequences of sin continue and have to be dealt with. The catechism affirms that sickness and suffering are both consequences of sin, while holding that they are not identical. A clear difference can be seen between the suffering caused by illness and that which is caused by injustice. Christ is pained by both but not in the same degree.

With a glance towards eternity, the introduction reminds us that, compared to the greatness of eternal glory for which they prepare us, the afflictions of the present time seem momentary and slight. And it goes further, for it says that it is part of God's plan that we should 'fight strenuously against all sickness and carefully seek the blessings of good health.' We should also be prepared 'to fill up what is lacking in Christ's sufferings for the salvation of the world as we look forward to creation's being set free in the glory of the children of God.' The expression 'making up what is lacking...' is from Colossians 1:24; the remainder comes from Romans 8:9–21. Sickness and the suffering associated with it is here given a new role, one which contributes to the 'groaning of creation' in its anticipation of what is to come. The idea derives partly from the Jewish and early Christian view that an allotted degree of suffering, termed the 'messianic woes', must be undergone before the coming of the Saviour and the final consummation. It must be said that the Pauline idea of filling up what is lacking in Christ's suffering remains an obscure one. It can be elucidated in terms of the relation of the head to the members but, given the sufficiency of the sacrifice of Calvary, it remains difficult to comprehend.

The sick are also described as having a role in the Church, reminding others of the essential or higher things and showing that mortal life in its entirety must be redeemed. The catechism recognises that sickness can incline a person in two directions. It can lead to deep pain, to despair, and even to revolt against God. Alternatively, it can lead to a reappraisal of one's life and provide the basis for a renewed search for God and a return to him.

Fighting sickness, *PCS* declares, is a communal venture. The sick are not the only ones to fight it and should not have to do it alone. Physicians, surgeons and others are called to use all available means to help the sick both physically and spiritually. The basis of this call is the commandment of God to visit the sick, for, the introduction says, 'Christ implied that those who visit the sick should be concerned for the whole person and offer both physical relief and spiritual comfort.'

Christ's own attitude to sickness and to the sick requires some further exploration before we can consider the sacramental ministry in the Catholic tradition. According to Matthew, Jesus cured every disease and every sickness among the people. The main categories listed in the Gospel are people afflicted with various diseases and pains, together with demoniacs, epileptics, and paralytics. All were cured (4:23–4). These miracles, which appear in the other Gospels as well, were interpreted as signs that God had visited his people (Luke 7:16) and that the Kingdom of God had drawn near. Jesus not only healed the physical ailments but also forgave sins (Mark 2:5–12). The catechism affirms that Jesus has come to heal human beings in their totality, soul and body. He is the physician needed by the sick (Mark 2:17), who also identifies himself with the sick. In the well-known passage from Matthew, the Son of Man says, 'I was sick and you visited me' (25:36). A number of translations render this as 'you took care of me'. The Greek verb *episkeptomai* conveys the sense of more than just an occasional visit; it is a visit undertaken with concern, with the purpose of offering comfort and relief. The sense of being involved in the continuing work of Christ, of manifesting his love for the sick, has been the constant driving force behind the efforts of the Church and of individual Christians to alleviate suffering of both body and soul.

There is no uniform way in which Jesus deals with the sick. Sometimes he looks for faith from the sick person. He uses various signs to bring about healing: for example, saliva and the imposition of hands (Mark 7:32–6; 8:22–5), and clay and washing (John 9:6–7). The sick realised that healing was to be found by touching him 'for power came out of him and healed them all' (Luke 6:19). In the sacraments, Christ continues to provide the opportunity for that healing touch.

Individual healing, important as it is, is not, however, the fullness of Christ's healing power. Matthew 8:17, quoting Isaiah 53:4, says he *took* our infirmities and *bore* our diseases. He did not heal all the sick of his day; the healings he did perform were signs of the Kingdom and a means of announcing the more radical healing brought about by his Easter victory over sin and death. He has not taken our suffering away but he has given it a new meaning such that those who suffer are made like him and are united to his own redemptive suffering.

It is this clear understanding of the nature of sickness that provides the basis for pastoral care in the Roman Catholic tradition. It involves a highly developed anthropology, in marked contrast to the *ASB*, and a hopefulness that has countered the more negative aspects of the medieval inheritance. The parish priest charged with pastoral care is to visit the faithful and their families, to share in their cares and sorrows, and to comfort them in the name of the Lord. Canon law requires him to help the sick and especially the dying, restoring them with the sacraments and, in due course, commending their souls to God. The canons do not refer to a ministry of healing other than by way of the sacrament of anointing.

The new catechism begins the section on healing by reminding us that Christ invited his disciples to take up the cross and follow him. In following him, his disciples acquired a new regard for sickness and for the sick. Associated with Jesus in his life of poverty and service, the disciples also participated in his ministry to the sick. Mark records that the Twelve went out two by two and 'proclaimed that all should repent. They cast out many demons, and anointed with oil many who were sick and cured them' (Mark 6:12–13). In the longer ending of Mark, Jesus says of his disciples that they will use his name to cast out demons and that they will lay their hands on the sick and they will recover (Mark 16:17–18). These signs – exorcisms and healings – are perceived as an important part of the Church's ministry, signs of the presence of God in Church and ministry. The catechism also points to the gift of healing among the gifts of the Holy Spirit but acknowledges that even the most intense prayer may not always obtain healing for all who are sick and for all types of sickness. It recalls the words of Paul and the assurance he received: 'My grace is sufficient for you, for power is made perfect in weakness' (2 Corinthians 12:9).

The Church has, nevertheless, received from the Lord the command to heal the sick (Matthew 10:8). She believes in the living presence of Christ, physician of souls and bodies, and sees his presence most certainly in the sacraments and especially in the Eucharist, the bread which gives eternal life, the reception of which is clearly linked by Paul to bodily health (1 Corinthians 11:30). But, of course, the Church also has a rite of the sick, attested by St James in apostolic times with an assurance that the prayer of faith with anointing will save the sick, the Lord will raise them up, and their sins will be forgiven (James 5:14–15). It is this sacrament, therefore, that carries the full weight for the Church's ministry of the command to heal but it is placed in a wider context, the ministry to the sick of the whole Christian community and especially of those qualified in medical practice.

The Sacrament of the Sick

The anointing of the sick is counted as one of the sacraments of the Church in the Catholic tradition. The *Revised Catechism* of the Church of England (1962) spoke of the sacramental ministry of healing and defined it as

> ...the ministry by which God's grace is given for the healing of spirit, mind, and body, in response to faith and prayer, by the laying on of hands, or by anointing with oil.

The catechism published in the American *Book of Common Prayer* (1979) deals specifically with unction:

> Unction is the rite of anointing the sick with oil, or the laying on of hands, by which God's grace is given for the healing of spirit, mind, and body.

The pairing of the laying-on of hands and anointing has given rise to some confusion in Anglican practice. Laying-on of hands is undoubtedly part of the Church's ministry to the sick. In an informal way anyone may lay hands upon another person and pray for them. In the formal sense, an authorised minister of the Church, ordained or lay, should perform the rite and those who have a specific charismatic gift of healing may join in at the minister's invitation. Within the Catholic tradition it is anointing with oil, and not the laying-on of hands, which may accompany anointing, which is the sacramental rite. The Church of England teaches that anointing is a ministry of the ordained priesthood, that the material element is pure olive oil which has been blessed, and that the method of administration is anointing with oil on the forehead in the sign of a cross, and that other parts of the body, notably the hands, may be anointed in addition. The *Roman Ritual* defines it in a very similar way:

> The celebration of this sacrament consists especially in the laying on of hands by the priests of the Church, the offering of the prayer of faith, and the anointing of the sick with oil made holy by God's blessing. This rite signifies the grace of the sacrament and confers it.

Sacramental theology has a traditional structure in which it asks questions about the recipient, minister, material element, etc., of the sacraments. The sections below follow just such a structure.

Who may receive the sacrament?

The sense of unction as a ministry of healing has to some extent been recovered; who then may receive sacramental anointing? *PCS* maintains it as the sacrament for the seriously sick; it is to be used more sparingly than laying-on of hands and prayer for the sick. If an illness is judged to be serious, threatening quality of life or life itself, then the sacrament may be reasonably administered. It is not just or even primarily for the dying. Among those who should certainly be anointed are the elderly when acute or chronic sickness notably weakens them, those about to receive surgery because of serious illness, and sick children. It is, however, a sacrament of faith and a child should be of a sufficient age to understand something of what is involved and to be strengthened by it. The dead are not to be sacramentally anointed, any more than they are to be baptised. The sacraments are for the living.

Who is the minister?

If we follow the American catechism we see that anointing is (a) a rite, and (b) a means by which God's grace is given for healing. Now sacraments are outward and visible signs, that is rites, of inward and spiritual grace. Grace is God's favour towards us, unearned and undeserved. By grace God forgives our sins, enlightens our minds, stirs our hearts and strengthens our wills. A rite requires a minister. The ministers of the sacraments have always been those whom God has called and ordained and whom the Church has commissioned, giving them authority as ministers of Word and sacraments. The efficacious sacramental word can only be pronounced by those who carry that authority. Charismatic gifts are of a different order, as the 1922 Doctrine Commission Report observed with truly prophetic insight. It called these gifts 'wider and more episodic activities of the Spirit'. The passage is worth quoting in full (the language is not inclusive):

The Spirit of Christ is at work throughout the body of

believers subduing all things to himself. But this does not mean that any member may perform any function indifferently, any more than every function of the human body can be performed indifferently by any limb. Each has its own function, and the one life of the body is expressed through the due performance by each of its own function. The official and ritual functions of the Church exist in order to express and mediate the life of Christ in his Body, alike in worship offered to the Father and in ministry to the needs of men; and for these functions an official Ministry is required, holding commission to act in the name of the whole Church. This necessity for the regular Ministry is not diminished by the fact that many laymen are effectual prophets and evangelists through whom the saving power of the life of Christ is expressed and mediated, sometimes with striking and enduring results. The distinctive functions of the Ministry, which, besides the regular preaching of the Gospel, include the continuous leadership of the people in worship, systematic teaching and pastoral care, would still be necessary even though 'all the Lord's people were prophets.' Moreover, the effective witness of Christian prophets and evangelists, either within the Ministry or without it, is given from within the Church, and is an expression of the continuous life of the Church which the regular Ministry of word and sacraments sustains from generation to generation.

The sacramental ministry to the sick rather than any form of charismatic healing belongs firmly in that continuous life.

The priest, also called presbyter, is the only proper minister of the anointing of the sick. A bishop can, of course, exercise all the functions of a priest. It follows from the nature of the cure of souls that the primary and proper minister will be the priest who has the cure of souls and who in consequence has the right, duty and obligation of administering the sacrament to those entrusted to his or her pastoral care. In other words, sacramental ministry is and must be closely linked to pastoral care. The priest is expected to pray for the sick and to have faith in God's healing power communicated by the rite of anointing.

What is the right approach to the sacrament?
In other words, what is the recipient's part in this? Faith is a prerequisite for the reception of the sacrament. The older rites of the visitation of the sick stressed the need to maintain the sick person in faith and, where necessary, to recall the individual by the reading of Scripture, by rehearsing a form of creed, or by prayer, to a recognition both of God's grace and of the redemptive aspects of suffering already noted here. This can be difficult. We are broadly agreed that suffering is bad and to be avoided. We do not deliberately cause other people to suffer. We give money to relieve suffering. Yet having suffered in a variety of ways, we tend to recognise that we are who we are precisely because of that experience which has reminded us of our mortality, frailty and fallibility. The collect for Lent 3 in the *ASB* and in the new calendar provisions says of Jesus that 'he went not up to joy but first he suffered pain, and entered not into glory before he was crucified'. It goes on to ask that

we, walking in the way of the cross, may find it none other than the way of life and peace. Though it may seem to echo medieval ideas about suffering, it is not a medieval collect nor even the product of Archbishop Cranmer's pen. It was written in the 1880s by the American priest and liturgist William Reed Huntington as the collect for the Monday in Holy Week for the 1892 American Prayer Book. He drew the line quoted from the exhortation in the Visitation of the Sick in the 1662 Prayer Book. It says: 'And there should be no greater comfort to Christian persons, than to be made like unto Christ, by suffering patiently adversities, troubles and sicknesses. For he himself went not up to joy but first he suffered pain . . .'. So, says the exhortation, our way to eternal joy is to suffer here with Christ. This is reminiscent of a dialogue that St Francis had with an amazed Brother Leo. Francis lists those things that the friars might achieve which would not bring perfect joy. For example:

> Brother Leo, says Francis, even if a Friar Minor gives sight to the blind, heals the paralysed, drives out devils, gives hearing back to the deaf, makes the lame walk, and restores speech to the dumb, and what is still more, brings back to life a man who has been dead for days, write that perfect joy is not in that.

When Leo asks where perfect joy is to be found, Francis gives a collection of terrible things that could happen to them – being made to stand out in the rain and snow, cold and hungry, being cursed and insulted, being beaten, and much more besides – and says that if they endure all those evils and insults and blows with joy and patience, reflecting that they must accept and bear the sufferings of the blessed Christ patiently for love of him – 'Oh,' says Francis, 'Brother Leo write: that is perfect joy!'

We have here a strong strand in the Christian understanding of existence and of discipleship which, like contempt for the world and apostolic poverty, is largely ignored at the moment. Yet if we are to make sense of suffering, sickness and healing, we must take notice of it because ultimately it stands in very close relation to the paschal mystery. As the American liturgist Thomas Talley so wisely wrote:

> The passion of Christ, his agony and death, was not a divine *lapsus* nor was it a defeat of his holy will. Rather, the holiness of his will, the utter otherness of his will, is revealed in that agony and bloody sweat, that cross and passion, that precious death and burial, as much as by his mighty resurrection and glorious ascension.

Suffering is not, therefore, entirely bad and to be avoided. Our disposition as we approach the sacrament of the sick must include submission to God as well as faith in his healing power, never forgetting that death itself is also victory.

The 'matter' of the sacrament: the use of oil
Olive oil is the proper 'matter', the material element, of the sacrament of anointing. Pope Paul VI allowed the use of other oils derived from plants in those parts

of the world where olive oil is unobtainable or difficult to obtain. This is certainly not the case in Britain today. It would be inappropriate to use synthetic oils – such as baby oil or even the so-called essential oils used in aromatherapy – because the olive and its oil have a special significance in nature and in Scripture. From the freshly plucked olive leaf in the dove's mouth when it returned to the ark to the two olive trees and the two lampstands in Zechariah, which reappear in the Revelation to John, the olive makes a frequent appearance in the Hebrew Scriptures. It is assumed that there are olive orchards in the Promised Land and that the oil pressed from the fruit is used for anointing (Deuteronomy 28:40). Israel is described as 'a green olive tree, fair with goodly fruit' (Jeremiah 11:16). Apart from several references to the Mount of Olives, the olive is only mentioned once in the Gospels, in the parable of the unjust steward in Luke 16:6, but in Romans 11:16–24 Paul draws some of his basic imagery to describe the relation of Jews and Gentiles from the contrast between the wild and cultivated olive and the way in which both may be used to improve fruitfulness.

The problem, well known to modern Christianity, of transition from one culture to another is found with the spread of Christianity across Europe. For its cultivators, the olive tree is synonymous with civilisation itself and expressive of the highest human ideals. The olive belongs to the Mediterranean area and will not grow in northern latitudes. In consequence, it was never cultivated in England. In contrast with the

Mediterranean people, who used olive oil and owned an olive tree or a share of one, the peoples of northern Europe ate butter and the peasants kept cows. Like pepper or spices, olive oil was a luxury item in north-western Europe, but this was the heartland of the new medieval Christian society and northern churchmen – and that is what we still are – insisted that liturgical anointings be done with olive oil. Northern European society was prepared to pay the price for that insistence.

If we ask, then, whether some other oil could be used for anointing rather than or in preference to olive oil we are asking a complex and difficult question. The olive comes with a rich symbolic and mythic inheritance (and the luxury olive oils of the supermarket shelf reinforce this). As we move from a culture in which the olive is native to one where it is not, we need to identify the contents of this inheritance and to ask which elements need to be maintained. Although a few people favour baby oil and its equivalents, most would rightly resist the substitution of the synthetic for the natural. Objection to a change from the olive to other vegetable oils or to animal fats native to a specific culture is more complicated. The meaning of a symbol in liturgy derives from that symbol's relation to the other symbols that make up the liturgical and sacramental whole, the rite as it is performed. The olive draws its full sacramental significance both from the place and use of oil and from its quite specific relation to Christ, the Anointed One.

The place of oil and wine in the western Christian tradition is defined in part by that body of teaching, ordered and created in the fertile theological discourse of the twelfth-century schools, that we call sacramental theology. Initial attempts to provide a common understanding of the Church's rites were largely allegorical. In common with later theologians, these early efforts adhered to the principle enunciated by Augustine of Hippo (354–430) that sacraments ought to have a certain resemblance to those things of which they are the sacraments. Hugh of St Victor (d. 1142) defined a sacrament as 'a corporeal or material element set before the senses without, representing by similitude and signifying by institution and containing by sanctification some invisible and spiritual grace.' So we need some matter – bread, wine, water, oil – that is similar to what the sacrament is doing – feeding, washing, healing – to which added value and meaning is given by divine institution and which, by some form of blessing, conveys the grace which is not visible nor material but invisible and spiritual. We can say of oil that it has natural qualities and that these are similar to the overflowing grace of the Holy Spirit. We can say that Christ instituted anointing both by his own anointing with the Spirit at his baptism in Jordan and by sending out the disciples to anoint the sick. The word of blessing or consecration is added to the oil, and so a sacrament is made. This initial definition was refined by Peter Lombard (c. 1100–60), who made the sacrament as a whole – in this case the whole process of anointing with oil along with prayers and the laying-on of hands – rather than just the material element – the oil – the efficacious sign, that is the sign that does what it looks as if it is doing. In the writings of St Thomas Aquinas (c. 1225–74), the sacramental correspondence is developed still further. The sacramental sign is seen as conforming to some aspect of the sanctifying work of Christ, as being appropriate to the needs of humanity made up of body and soul, or of material and spiritual elements, and as conveying the specific meaning of the material sign by the use of words.

In the ritual context, the material sign has priority. Here the allegorical method searches for the ways in which the visible manifests the invisible. Citing the Epistle to the Romans – 'Ever since the world began God's invisible attributes . . .have been visible to the eye of reason in the things he has made' (Romans 1:20) – Amalarius of Metz (c. 750–850/1) seeks out that which the olive, its fruit and its oil, may reveal. He quotes Isidore of Seville (c. 560–636) who, in the *Etymologia*, a fascinating but unreliable collection of derivations of words, refers to the olive as *arbor pacis insignis* (the famous tree of peace) and speaks of the richness of the fruit and the refreshment it brings to the sick. Like the hymn *O Redemptor*, long sung at the blessing of the oils on Maundy Thursday (the Chrism Mass), Isidore draws attention to the relation between the olive and light, obvious from its need for constant sunshine if it is to bear fruit. Amalarius cites Augustine who calls the visible oil a sign of the invisible oil; as the natural oil brings physical health so the invisible supernatural oil conveys the inner health appropriate to each type of anointing. Typology is used as well as allegory and prayers for the blessing of the oils and commentaries upon them draw on the symbolism of the dove's mouth as a type of the gift to come in Christ and find in the anointing of Aaron by Moses a foreshadowing of the baptism of Jesus by John and his spiritual anointing. This then is the rich symbolic matrix of the olive and its oil, and one must ask how any other oil, synthetic, vegetable or animal, could possibly convey this complex and multi-layered meaning.

In the Middle Ages attempts were clearly made in the West to use other oils. The substitution of nut-oil and butter was proscribed by the ecclesiastical authorities. Thomas Aquinas addresses the question with regard both to the material element in anointing (oil) and in the Eucharist (bread and wine). On confirmation, he asks whether chrism – olive oil with balsam added, consecrated by the bishop – is suitable matter for this sacrament. In his reply he picks up Hugh's ideas of representation, signification, and sanctification. He says that no other oil has the properties that signify the Holy Spirit in the way that olive oil does, for 'the olive tree itself with branches always green, signifies the newness and mercy of the Holy Spirit'. Aquinas holds that *oleum* means *olive oil* and that other pressed liquids are called *oil* because of a likeness to *oleum olivarum*. So the oil signifies the grace of the Holy Spirit and because Christ received this grace in its fullness he is said to have been anointed with the oil of gladness. Aquinas cannot, however, argue directly from the Gospels, for Christ was anointed with the Holy Spirit and not with oil, and he did not explicitly institute anointing at confirmation. The same is true of anointing the sick but the ultimate sacramental principle is surely that sacraments exist for people and not people for sacraments.

The oil must be blessed, ordinarily by the bishop. In the absence of oil blessed by the bishop a priest may bless it. Good pastoral practice requires that the oil be replaced at least annually, that it be carried in a suitable container, and that, after use, the remaining oil is returned to the place where it is normally kept with proper respect. A small oil container used to carry it to the sick is best filled with cotton wool that is then soaked in the oil; this makes administration easier.

How is the sacrament administered?

The priest uses one of the forms provided in *Ministry to the Sick* (1983) or in *A Manual for Ministry to the Sick* (1997) or some other collection of rites, which include a psalm and a short lesson. It may also include or be preceded by confession and absolution. The laying-on of hands with prayer for healing precedes the anointing. The priest then dips his or her thumb into the oil and makes the sign of the cross on the forehead and, if desired, on the hands. The words said at the anointing are spoken once only and are followed by a prayer for healing. *PCS* adds this rubric:

Depending upon the culture and traditions of the place, as well as the condition of the sick person, the priest may also anoint additional parts of the body, for example, the area of pain or injury. He does not repeat the sacramental form.

In deciding, in consultation with the sick person and those caring for them, the minister must guard against any suggestion of exploitation or abuse, allow the sick person their full and proper dignity, and respect their physical person. It is generally wise to limit the anointing to head and hands.

After the anointing, the oil is wiped off using cotton wool or tissue and this is then burned if at all possible.

What is the effect of the sacrament?
Catholic teaching puts salvation before physical healing. A return to physical health may follow the reception of the sacrament but only if it will be beneficial to the sick person's salvation. What the sacrament does is to give the grace of the Holy Spirit which helps the person physically and spiritually, strengthens them and reinforces their trust in God, and reduces anxiety about death. The primary focus of the sacrament is spiritual well-being but so close is the connection between spirit and matter, between soul and body, that what nourishes the one must have a beneficial effect on the other. The sacrament also amplifies that union with Christ in his suffering which has already been mentioned. The person receiving the Church's ministrations is united more closely to the Body of Christ, not only receiving the benefits of

membership but, at the same time, contributing to the life of the Church by suffering with Christ. In the event of terminal illness, the anointing prepares the person for the last journey. It is the *sacramentum exeuntium*, the sacrament of the dying, as well as the sacrament of healing.

By what other ways does the Church minister to the sick?

The responsibility of care for the sick is laid by Christ on all baptised Christians. Kindness to the sick and works of charity and mutual aid have always had a special place in the Church's life. The family and friends of the sick have a special responsibility, not least in informing the parish priest when sickness gets worse, and in preparing the sick to receive the sacraments. The sacrament of the sick itself clearly includes the prayer of faith and intercession for the sick, privately and corporately. At the Eucharist and in other acts of worship, such prayer and intercession are an obligation laid on the Christian community. Sick people are not somehow outside the Church and they can be enabled to minister to the Church as well as receiving the Church's ministry. They recall us to an awareness of the inevitability of death in a disordered creation; they remind us of our mortality and frailty; they provide us with opportunities to continue Christ's own concern for the sick and the dying.

Conclusion

Ministry to the sick is commanded by Christ himself who, as the Gospels show, provided a standard by which our attitude and practice are to be judged. Both in Jesus' own time and subsequently in the life of the early Church oil was used to anoint the sick. They were also prayed for and the elders of the church laid hands on them. In the Middle Ages anointing the sick was recognised as one of the seven sacraments and called extreme unction. It tended to be one of the last rites administered to Christians as they approached death.

Though for different reasons, this ministry declined in both the Anglican and Roman Catholic Churches. Within Anglicanism the initiative for the recovery of a full sacramental ministry to the sick began towards the end of the nineteenth century but it has still not gained a recognised and normative position in the life of most parishes. In the Roman Catholic Church the renewal of anointing was part of the liturgical reform that followed the Second Vatican Council.

Sacramental ministry is deficient if it does not include anointing the sick. Careful catechesis is needed to ensure that Christians understand the importance of informing their parish priest when they are ill, not merely to explain their absence from worship, but so that they may be prayed for, brought communion at home, and, if the illness is serious or life-threatening, receive anointing with the laying-on of hands and prayer.

This is not just a matter of good sacramental practice. Our understanding of what it means to be human, to be created and redeemed, and to fulfil in our lives that humanity of which Christ is the great exemplar, requires us to address the problems of sickness, pain, suffering and the inevitability of death. Christianity focuses more on the saving of souls than the healing of bodies but in life the two are inseparable. We are a single unity of spirit and matter and the Christian belief is in resurrection of the body and not in immortality of the (disembodied) soul. Bodies are important. Matter is not evil. The sacraments, in their use of material elements, testify to this and the anointing of the sick amply demonstrates that God's salvific word is addressed to us in the fullness and entirety of our humanity.

Questions

Humanity, Health and Sickness
1. Do you think that the nature of our humanity can be defined in a universal way? Will it always reflect the cultural, social and historical position of the person defining it?

2. Archaeology offers evidence of the way ordinary people lived in biblical times and gives a different picture of humanity. Is the view offered in the Bible too limited?

3. Are 'the sick' really a clearly identifiable and separate group of people to be visited, prayed for, cared for?

4. Rites for the dying were crucially important in the Middle Ages but are rarely practised now. Should we seek to restore the cycle of confession, communion and anointing for those approaching death?

The Anglican Tradition
1. Do we perceive the world in the same way as they did in the seventeenth century? Do we see life as uncertain and subject to 'sudden perils, diseases and sickness'?

2. Is sickness a consequence of sin? Does God use sickness in order to punish?

3. Can you find a clear understanding of our humanity in *The Alternative Service Book*? If not, why do you think it is absent? If so, how does it relate to that in *The Book of Common Prayer*?

4. Must there be a conflict between 'charismatic' healing and the 'eldership' view?

The Roman Catholic Tradition

1. Is the Roman Catholic understanding of sickness and death compatible with that found in modern medicine?

2. Consider the language in which we talk about 'being poorly', 'being ill' and 'being sick'. Is there a difference of understanding implicit, or perhaps explicit, in the language we use?

3. In what sense can it be said that Christ's sufferings are not yet completed?

4. Is the strength to bear sickness as good as being healed? Is it better to minister out of weakness rather than from strength?

The Sacrament of the Sick

1. When would you consider it better to lay on hands rather than to anoint? Should a minister ever refuse anointing?

2. People often ask if a dead newborn child may be baptised. Should it be an absolute rule that sacraments are for the living?

---

3. Should lay people be permitted to anoint the sick? What difference would it make?

4. Does it really make a difference if baby oil is used to anoint?

5. There is a good deal of concern today about positions in which the powerful and the vulnerable meet. This concern extends to the pastoral relationship where the priest is seen as powerful and the sick person as weak. What rules should be observed to maintain this as a beneficial relationship?

6. Can we measure the effectiveness of a sacrament? What criteria would we employ?

Further Reading and Resources

The background to anointing is set out in Martin Dudley and Geoffrey Rowell, *The Oil of Gladness* (London: SPCK, 1993).

The sections of the *Catechism of the Catholic Church* concerned with ministry to the sick 1499–1532. (I have used the French text in preference to the English version.)

Liturgical texts for ministering to the sick are to be found in a number of collections. The official Church of England texts are in *Ministry to the Sick* (Clowes, 1983) and *Ministry at the Time of Death* (Church House Publishing, 1991). Roman Catholic rites are in *Pastoral Care of the Sick* (London: Geoffrey Chapman, 1983). There are a variety of prayers for use with the sick together with forms for confession, for anointing the sick, and for commending the dying in Martin Dudley (ed.), *A Manual for Ministry to the Sick* (London: SPCK, 1997).

The Anglican Charles Gusmer has written extensively and definitively on the subject. His standard work is *And You Visited Me; Sacramental Ministry to the Sick and Dying* (revised, New York: Pueblo, 1986). A useful companion to *PCS* is T. Coyle, *Christian Ministry to the Sick* (London: Geoffrey Chapman, 1986).